Guide To Lincoln Castle

W. K. Morton And Sons Publisher

In the interest of creating a more extensive selection of rare historical book reprints, we have chosen to reproduce this title even though it may possibly have occasional imperfections such as missing and blurred pages, missing text, poor pictures, markings, dark backgrounds and other reproduction issues beyond our control. Because this work is culturally important, we have made it available as a part of our commitment to protecting, preserving and promoting the world's literature. Thank you for your understanding.

Castle Gateway.

LINCOLN:
ED BY W. K. MORTON & SONS, LTD., 290, HIGH STREET.
1906.

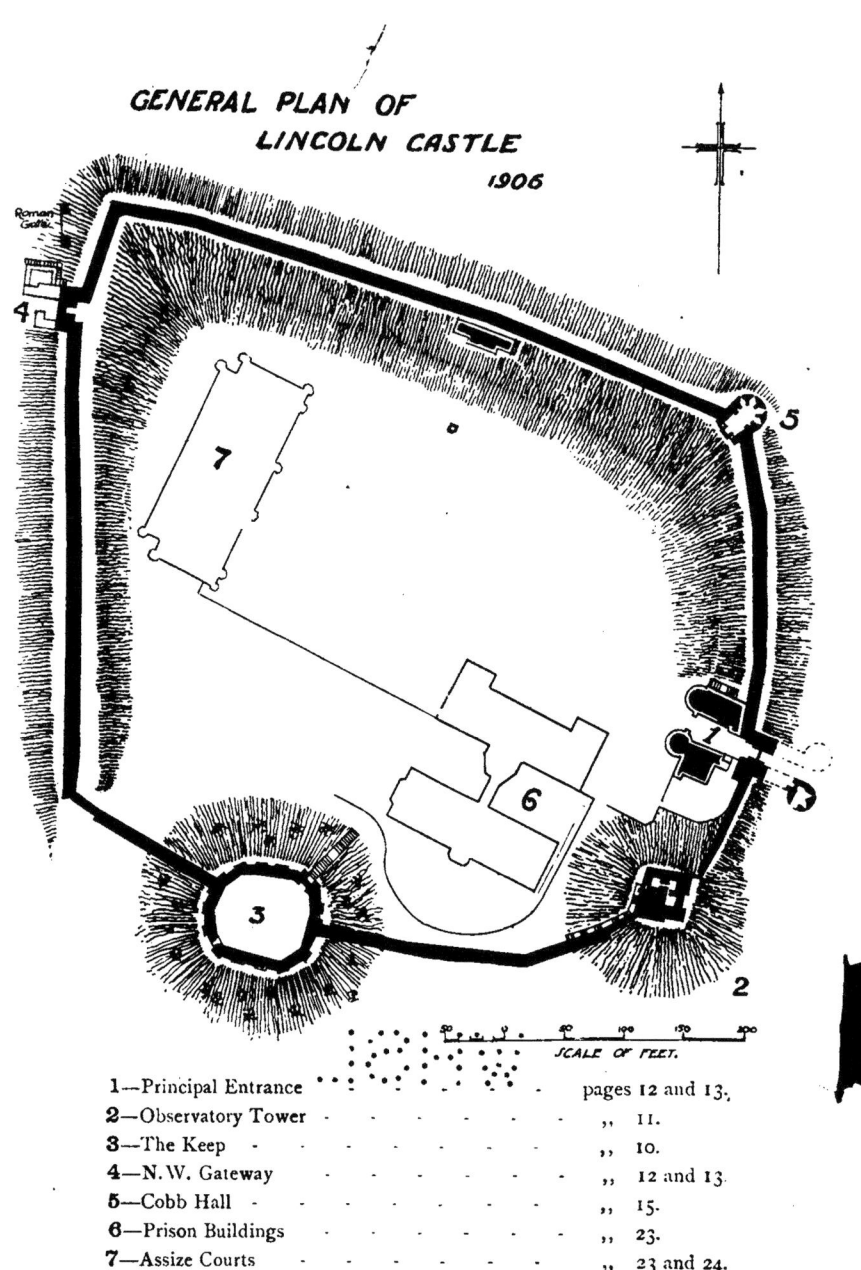

GENERAL PLAN OF
LINCOLN CASTLE
1906

SCALE OF FEET.

1—Principal Entrance — pages 12 and 13.
2—Observatory Tower — ,, 11.
3—The Keep — ,, 10.
4—N.W. Gateway — ,, 12 and 13.
5—Cobb Hall — ,, 15.
6—Prison Buildings — ,, 23.
7—Assize Courts — ,, 23 and 24.

Castle Itinerary.

The figures in parentheses refer to the pages upon which fuller details are to be found.

THE principal entrance (pp. 12-13) is upon the eastern side of the Castle enclosure, and is approached from Castle Hill. This gateway is of Norman date, with pointed arch and flanking turrets of the Edwardian period. Within the small court is a beautiful fifteenth century oriel window (p. 14), brought from John o' Gaunt's Palace below the hill; here also is a fragment from the first of the Eleanor Crosses formerly standing near Cross o' Cliff Hill at the southern end of the city (p. 14).

Following the line of walling to the left or southward, the visitor reaches the Observatory Tower (p. 11) situate at the top of a lofty mound. The lower walling is of Norman work, other parts are Edwardian, and the remainder is comparatively modern. From the top of this tower may be seen a splendid prospect of the city and the surrounding country.

Near to the centre of the southern wall is the Norman Keep (p. 10), erected upon the summit of a very high hill-mound. This is a fine example of a "shell" keep, the walls of which were originally much loftier than at present; internally it is twelve-sided and has an inner and an outer doorway, and at about 10 feet above the floor level it has two small chambers at the points of junction with the main walling. Within the walls of the Keep are the graves of prisoners executed within the Castle, and of debtors and others who have died in gaol.

At the north-western corner of the Castle is the second or western Norman entrance (pp. 12-13); like the eastern gateway, it was formerly two storeys high, it has also a lofty semi-circular archway—now blocked; two small windows and a doorway remain in the upper portion, and ruins of extensive outworks or towers can be seen from the outside. Near the north-western corner of the Castle, and in the western mound, outside the walls, were found, in 1836, the remains of the western gateway of the Roman city, Lindum Colonia (pp. 6, 25).

In the northern and the western walls, both inside and out, may be seen very good examples of "herring-bone" work, *i.e.*, courses of thin stone laid obliquely.

At the north-eastern corner of the Castle is the tower known as "Cobb Hall" (p. 15), from the practice of cobbing or beating prisoners here. This tower is of early fourteenth century or Edwardian date, and has two storeys, each vaulted, and very narrow deeply recessed windows. Remains of mediæval carving by a prisoner, Thomas Godard, may be seen on the left jamb of the eastern window in the basement (p. 15).

Up to the year 1860 the hanging in public of prisoners condemned to death took place upon the roof of this tower, from which a magnificent view of the Minster front may be obtained.

The walling of the Castle is of Norman date, about 10 feet thick and about 20 feet high, erected upon an earthen mound of varying heights; the two hill-mounds are each about 40 feet high. The extent of the Castle, within the walls, is about $6\frac{1}{4}$ acres, and inclusive of mound and former moat about 14 acres.

With regard to the general construction of the walling, the materials consist chiefly of local oolite in roughly coursed rubble; the Keep, the Observatory Tower, and all the later work being of wrought ashlar.

The red brick building erected in 1787 (p. 23), was formerly the Governor's residence and debtors' prison. The front portion is now used for the Petty Sessions of the Lincoln Divisions of Lindsey and Kesteven, and at the back may be seen the prisoners' chapel and the cells, built in 1846.

The County Hall, with Assize Courts, at the further end of the Castle Yard, was built in 1826, from the design of Sir Robert Smirke, and the Grand Jury Room on the upper floor contains several portraits of County Magistrates and others.

Castle Guide.

THE Castle of Lincoln is situate upon the brow of a lofty hill, which, because of its commanding position, would in pre-historic times doubtless be both inhabited and fortified, though few traces of such early occupation are at present known.

Roman Occupation.

Historical Lincoln dates from the time of the conquest of England by the Romans, who gave to their new settlement the title Lindum. It is called "Lindum Colina" by the Ravenna Geographer of the seventh century, and "Lindocolena Civitas" by the Venerable Bede, who died A.D. 735. These forms make it clear that for the first part of their name the Romans retained the word "Lindum"; *i.e.*, hill-fort (dun), by the deep pool (linn), which had appropriately been bestowed upon the locality by the ancient Celtic inhabitants. Professor Freeman considered the modern form "Lincoln" to be equivalent to "Lin(dum) Colonia", his words being: "In its ending it proclaims the rank which Lindum held among Roman cities . . . the city by the Witham keeps her earliest name as well as the title of her Roman rank, and proclaims herself through the whole of her long history as the colony of Lindum." [1]

The importance of this site would be evident to the experienced eyes of the Roman conquerors, who having seized and fortified it, founded thereon their permanent town or station; numerous and extensive remains of the Roman occupation exist in all parts of the present city, and at its northern entrance the Roman gateway, known as "Newport Arch," still spans, as of old, the Roman "Ermine Street," and near at hand the lines of Roman walling and moat are visible.

In conformity with the prevalent custom this station was divided into four equal parts by the usual intersecting main roads, the Minster and its adjuncts being subsequently built in the south-eastern quarter of the Roman town, and the Castle being erected in the south-western section.

The western gateway of the Roman station was found in the year 1836 beneath the outer slope of the

---

(1) This is the generally accepted explanation, but it is not unquestioned, and other authorities see in the second syllable the Latin "collina," an adjectival form from "collis," a hill.

Castle earthworks at a point midway between the western gateway and the north-western angle of the mound, and the direction of this embankment was evidently so altered that the foundation of the Castle walling might not be weakened at this point. Further remains of Roman walling are believed to exist within other portions of the mounds and moat.

Roman remains have occasionally been discovered within the Castle area; for instance, in 1788, a vessel of black pottery was found 14 feet below the surface of the ground, and it is illustrated in "Archæologia," Vol. IX., plate 24, a note as to the discovery having been communicated to the Society of Antiquaries by Thomas Pownall, Governor of Massachusetts, 1757-60, a well-known archæologist; and in 1846, when the new gaol was built at the back or southern side of the older prison, a tesselated pavement was laid bare at a depth of 12 feet below the surface; this pavement measured 17 feet 4 inches in length by 12 feet in width, and extended over a hypocaust, and, as a layer of cinders was found immediately above the pavement, it has been inferred that the building of which it formed a part was destroyed by fire. A drawing of this pavement, which was made by G. J. Wigley at the time of the discovery, passed into the possession of Mr. E. L. Grange, of Grimsby, and a chromo-lithograph of it was published in the first volume of "Lincolnshire Notes and Queries."

Saxons and Danes.

When the Romans retired from England the country was gradually occupied by the Saxons, and we catch glimpses of Lincoln in the pages of the Venerable Bede, who relates the fact that early in the seventh century the Missionary Bishop, Paulinus, converted Blecca, Governor of the City of Lincoln, and all his family.

Towards the end of the eighth, and during the two following centuries, the Danes invaded the land, and effected many settlements; Lincoln was one of their strongest and most important positions.

Mr. G. T. Clark, in his "Mediæval Military Architecture in England," discusses the origin of Lincoln Castle, and considers it probable that the massive earthworks found here were constructed in the period subsequent to the departure of the Romans, and prior to the coming of the Normans, and that this stronghold was, by order of William the Conqueror, developed into the structure ultimately known as Lincoln Castle; some modern archæologists, however, dissent from this view, and are of opinion that the earthworks are entirely of Norman date.

The extent and outlines of the Castle enclosure were, without doubt, considerably affected by the then existing remains of Roman Lindum. The Castle was bounded on the northern side by the Roman Street running east and west, and the direction and length of the southern and western sides were modified to suit the respective positions of the Roman walls.

The original fortress consisted of two lofty detached conical hill-mounds on the southern face, and a long line of lower embankment which encloses the courtyard towards the north; the detached mounds were each encircled by a moat, the whole area was surrounded by a deep dry ditch, and the defences of the place were increased and strengthened by the erection of strong timber buildings and stockades upon the summits of the steep-sloped earthworks. Fortresses formed during the ninth or tenth centuries, whether in England or in Normandy, were generally of this type, but Mr. Clark points out that Lincoln Castle is especially interesting as having two fortified hill-mounds instead of the single one more usually found.

The line of the earthen mound varies in height from about 15 to 25 feet, and in width at base from 150 to 200 feet. The two detached mounds are each about 40 feet high, and the "Keep" mound has at the top a diameter of about 100 feet. The Castle measures about 230 yards over all from east to west, and from north to south about 170 yards within the walls, and when the moat was in a perfect state its entire area was probably 13 or 14 acres.

Norman Work.

After the visit of William the Conqueror to Lincoln in 1068, a clearance was made of numerous buildings which had been erected upon or within the encircling mounds and moat. This fact is recorded in Domesday Book, which states that "166 dwellings (*mansiones*) were destroyed on account of the Castle." The military position was rendered temporarily secure by the strengthening and repair of the defective stockades, and when, as at York and Cambridge and other places, the erection of a permanent fortress was commenced, the lines of the new walling were undoubtedly made to follow upon, and co-incide with, those of the former palisading, the bottom timbers of which would in all probability be embedded in the base of the walling to form and to strengthen the needed foundations.

In Norman times the buildings of the Castle consisted of two towers, (the Keep, and the Observatory tower), two gateways, and the enclosing wall of the courtyard; the third tower, known as "Cobb Hall," is of the Edwardian period, and there is no evidence that a Norman structure ever existed upon this site.

At the time of the Domesday Survey Lincoln contained 1150 houses, and during the Conqueror's reign it had greatly increased in wealth and importance, for that record states that whereas in the time of King Edward the Confessor it used to render £20 to the King and £10 to the Earl, it then (*i.e.* at the completion of the Survey in 1086), rendered £100, divided between the King and the Earl, and this growth was probably due to the security which resulted from the garrisoning of the Castle, and the walling-in and fortifying of the whole of the City.

The Keep, (Lucy Tower).

The Keep is irregular in plan, having fifteen sides externally and twelve internally, and is built half within and half without the lines of the southern walling of the Castle; it is an excellent example of a "Shell" Keep, which was a kind of roofless tower, the walls of which enclosed a series of narrow buildings surrounding a central space or court open to the sky. The walls of the Keep, which are now only about 15 feet high were originally much more lofty, and they vary in thickness from about 6 to 8 feet. At a height of about 10 feet above the ground floor level, and within the thickness of the walling, are two small chambers; that on the eastern side, with remains of vaulted roofing, was possibly a chapel; the other, in the western wall, was a "garde-robe" or closet.

The Keep has two doorways, the northern one, which is within the Castle enclosure, gives access by a lofty flight of steps from the Castle court below; the other doorway which is outside the line of the southern walling was very difficult of approach because of the steepness of the mound up which an enemy must clamber; the doors were secured by wooden bars across the openings, and no trace of portcullis is apparent at either of them; the stonework of both has been extensively renewed.

In some ancient records the Keep is called the "Lucy Tower," and it was so named because it was fortified by Lucy, Countess of Chester, an heiress of Saxon descent; she was grand-daughter of Algar, Earl of Mercia, who was a son of the celebrated Earl Leofric and his wife the Lady Godiva. Lucy was married first to Roger de Romara, and, after his death, to Ranulph Meschines, Earl of Chester; by the former husband she was mother of William de Romara, Earl of Lincoln, and the issue of her second marriage was Ranulph de Gernons, Earl of Chester.

On the Pipe Roll for the second year of King John, (A.D. 1200), £20 is recorded to have been expended on the reparation of the *new tower* (*i.e.*, the Lucy Tower), and of the prison of the Castle; and in 1225 the Sheriff of Lincoln was ordered to repair the gate of the Castle facing St. Mary's Church, (*i.e.* the Church of St. Mary Magdalen), the Lucy Tower, and the barbican.

Observatory Tower.

Upon the south-eastern mound is the "Observatory" Tower, and it is so called from the fact that a former Governor who was interested in astronomy placed telescopes and other instruments there. This tower is rectangular in plan and is about 40 feet long by 25 feet wide; its lower portion only is Norman, other parts of the work date from the fourteenth century, and the circular turret, which gives the name to this tower, was added about a hundred years ago.

In the southern main wall and at the foot of the south-eastern or Observatory mound may be seen the remains of a small doorway of late Norman work.

Gateways.

The Castle has two gateways: the one situate near the centre of the eastern wall opened into the Bail (*i.e.* the area comprised within the jurisdiction of the Constable of the Castle), and the other, in the western wall near to the north-western corner of the Castle, gave access to the open field, and also to the "Battle Piece" belonging to the Castle domain. The eastern gateway being nearest to the streets and thoroughfares of the City is still, as of old, the chief entrance to the Castle and is now the only one available, the western gateway or sallyport being disused, and the approach and archway blocked; both gateways are of Norman date and are deeply recessed, having plain square massive jambs and semi-circular moulded arches, each about 14 feet in width. The eastern gateway has its Norman work concealed by later additions, and the portcullis groove is hidden and blocked by the woodwork framing of the modern doors; at the western gateway, however, the groove for the portcullis is visible, also the rebate or recess for holding and securing the ancient ponderous doors; the surface of the ground here has been much raised and the archway therefore is greatly reduced in height.

The western gateway has two small windows in the upper stage, and it has also at the same level, for access to outworks and battlements, a narrow doorway, 2 feet 4 inches wide and 6 feet 6 inches high, with stone lintel or head beneath a plain semi-circular relieving arch. Both gateways were defended by barbican towers or out-works, and at the western one extensive remains of flanking walls may still be seen.

The Keep and the two fortified gateways were probably built before the end of the eleventh century, and further additions were made in the reign of King Stephen, who granted to Ranulph de Gernons, Earl of Chester, "a licence to fortify" one of the towers of the Castle.

Post-Norman Work.

Of later or post-Norman work there are to be found portions in the external facing of the principal entrance, also at the Observatory Tower, and at Cobb Hall, and at each may be seen good work of the fourteenth century or Decorated period of architecture.

Principal Entrance.

This entrance consists of the remains of a two-storey turreted gateway built in front of and above the earlier Norman work, the semi-circular archway being almost entirely concealed by a bold and massive Gothic arch, the inner rib of which is carried upon large moulded octagonal corbels; this arch supports at its apex the salient angle and splayed walling of the upper storey, the whole being flanked by two circular projecting turrets boldly corbelled out at base, and these contain the remains of two circular stairways which afforded access to the battlements.

The Castle approach was defended not only by the moat but also by outer or barbican towers, of which the lower portion of the southern one, with loopholes and other remains, can be seen in the cellar of the adjacent house, and the basement vaulting of the northern tower has been recently discovered upon the opposite side of the entrance roadway; formerly this gateway was still further defended by the usual moat and drawbridge upon the outer side of these two towers.

When excavations were made some fifteen years ago a lofty underground passage was revealed, which formed a connection between the northern barbican tower and the main walling of the Castle; in 1791 the barbican walls and towers being much decayed, were removed by order of the County Magistrates, but, whilst yet standing, these, with other features of the Castle were, in 1782, described by Edward King in the pages of "Archæologia."

Within the entrance gateway may be seen a beautiful oriel window, probably of early fifteenth century date, which originally formed part of the Palace of John o' Gaunt and his daughter, Joan, below the hill. It was re-erected here after its acquisition in 1849 by the first Earl Brownlow, Lord Lieutenant of the County; here also may be seen a fragment of a draped statue, the only remaining relic from the Eleanor Cross at Cross o' Cliff Hill near to the southern entrance of the City. This was the first of the series of Crosses erected by King Edward I. at the various places, twelve in number, where rested the body of Queen Eleanor during the funeral procession from Harby, in Nottinghamshire, where she died, to the final resting-place in Westminster Abbey.

Cobb Hall.

This tower, which is situate at the north-eastern angle of the Castle, is probably so named from the custom of "cobbing" prisoners here, *i.e.*, beating them with straps. Externally it is circular in plan, and consists of two storeys with vaulted roofs and deeply splayed loop-holes for light and defence. In the basement are two blocked doorways opening respectively towards the west and the south upon the top of the earthen mound; in one of the bays of this same storey there is a curious and spirited representation of a hunting scene skilfully carved by a prisoner whose name, "Thomas Godard," appears upon the stone; this work, which was probably executed in the fourteenth century, has unfortunately been damaged, but in the centre is a stag, at which an arrow has been discharged by a man, whose up-lifted hand can still be discerned; mutilated representations of a lion, an eagle, and another animal, each in vigorous action, may also be seen, likewise two trees conventionally shown. On the walls of the upper floor are three incised Calvary crosses of mediæval date.

Cobb Hall, and the additions to the entrance gateway and to the Observatory Tower were probably built in the early years of the fourteenth century, when Thomas, Earl of Lancaster, was Constable of the Castle.

Near the doorway of Cobb Hall, is a damaged and weather-beaten stone which is supposed to represent a lion, and to have been originally placed outside the northern pier of the principal entrance; the corresponding figure upon the southern pier is unfortunately lost.

Ownership and Administration of the Castle.

The Castle was anciently part of the Crown demesnes, and was held and administered by Constables by the service of Castle Ward, and of guarding the prisoners confined therein. The Constable held at the Castle Gate the Court Baron of the Manor of the Castle; he had also a Court Leet with Assize of Bread and Ale, and exercised and enjoyed other manorial rights and privileges.

Sieges in the Barons' Wars.

During the troubled reign of King Stephen, Lincoln was the scene of several conflicts. Ranulph de Gernons, Earl of Chester, obtained possession of the city and Castle, and held them on behalf of the Empress Matilda. Stephen thereupon marched against Lincoln and proceeded to invest the Castle. The Earl of Chester escaped, effected a junction with Robert, Earl of Gloucester, and came to the relief of the besieged, with the result that the royal army was routed, and Stephen himself was taken prisoner. This battle was fought on the 2nd February, 1141, and is sometimes called the "Joust of Lincoln."

Three years later Stephen again attacked Lincoln, this time also without success. Subsequently the Earl of Chester was made prisoner by the King, and was compelled to surrender Lincoln and his other strongholds as the condition of his ransom. This Ranulph, Earl of Chester, was the son of the Lucy, Countess of Chester, mentioned on page 11. He afterwards became reconciled with King Stephen, and was taken into favour and received from the King the city and Castle of Lincoln, until he should be restored to his lands and castles in Normandy, and until the Castle of Tickhill should be delivered to him, after which, he was to restore the city and Castle of Lincoln to the King, excepting his own tower which his mother had fortified.

In 1153 it was stipulated that the Castle should be put in charge of Jordan de Bussey as Governor, he taking oath that he would, after King Stephen's death, surrender it to Prince Henry (afterwards Henry II) or to whomsoever he should appoint.

Lady Nichola de la Haye, Governor of the Castle.

Richard de la Haye afterwards held the Castle in fee, and upon his death, Richard I granted it to Gerard de Camville, (or de Canvilla), who had married Nichola de la Haye, eldest daughter and co-heiress of the said Richard de la Haye.

After Gerard's death, his widow (who is described by Dugdale as "an eminent woman in her days,") held it at the will of King John, in time of war and in time of peace.

The Hundred Rolls, of the third and fourth years of Edward I (1275-6), record an interesting inquisition taken by twelve faithful men of the City of Lincoln. It happened, we read, that the lord the King John came to Lincoln, and the said Lady Nichola went out to the west part of the Castle, carrying the Castle keys in her hand, and met the said lord the King John, and offered the keys to him as her lord, saying that she was a woman of great age, and that she had sustained many labours and anxieties in the said Castle, and was unable to sustain them longer; and the lord the King John *sweetly* handed them back to her, begging her, if she pleased, to continue still longer, and so she had the custody of the Castle all the time of the life of King John. Another version of the inquisition, purporting to preserve the words actually used by the King, represents him as saying, " My beloved, I will that you shall still have custody of this Castle, until I shall otherwise order."

The Lady Nichola held the Castle until the fifteenth year of the reign of King Henry III (1231), when she betook herself to Swaneton, and there died. In addition to being Governor of the Castle of Lincoln, she held the office of Sheriff of Lincolnshire in the eighteenth year of King John and in the first and second years of King Henry III.

"The Fair of Lincoln," 19th May, 1217.

During the struggle between King John and the barons the city of Lincoln was captured by Gilbert de Gant, who was created Earl of Lincoln by Prince Louis of France, to whom the insurgent barons had offered the crown; but the Castle, which had been garrisoned by Fulk de Breauté in 1215, was held for the King by the Lady Nichola; the barons had vigorously assaulted it with engines of timber, but their efforts had been unavailing. The city was still in the hands of the insurgents at the time of John's death, and the siege of the Castle was continued; thereupon, William Marshall, Earl of Pembroke, the Regent, assisted by William de Longespée, Earl of Salisbury, and others, advanced to its relief: he directed a body of his troops, commanded by Fulk de Breauté, to enter the Castle by the postern gate which opened into the fields, and, having gained admittance, they straightway sallied forth and attacked the insurgents in the city, whilst the Regent's main army stormed one of the city gates. The rebels being thus simultaneously attacked from two quarters were utterly defeated, and so much spoil was captured that the conflict was termed the "Fair of Lincoln."

Other Governors and Constables of the Castle.

In 1225 the Sheriff of Lincolnshire was ordered to pay Jordan de Esseby, the Constable of the Castle, 100s. for works of the Castle, and in 1226 the Constable of Chester was ordered to let the Constable of Lincoln Castle, Osbert Giffard, have forty great pieces of timber in the park of Tunner for purposes of fortification.

In the reign of Henry III (1216-72) Philip de Lasceles was Constable for three years and more, and one Walter de Everum was his successor.

In the same reign William de Longspei (or Longespée), Earl of Salisbury, who has been already mentioned, was constituted Governor of the Castle, he was called Longespée, *i.e.* Long-sword, from the long sword which he usually wore; he went to the Holy Land and subsequently to Gascony; returning to England he died in 1226, and was succeeded by his son, William Longespée, who was also a Crusader, and who married Idonea, daughter of Richard de Camville, and grand-daughter of the Lady Nichola. This second William was killed whilst fighting against the Saracens at Damietta in the year 1250, and was succeeded by his son, who also bore the name William; after his decease in 1257 Queen Eleanor held the Castle of Lincoln and his other lands as guardian of his daughter Margaret until she was of full age. In course of time this Margaret was married to Henry de Lacy, Earl of Lincoln, who became Constable in right of his wife, and he is stated to have been in actual possession in the year 1276.

The Hundred Rolls, already quoted, record it as a grievance that Walter de Bek, Constable of the Castle, (acting by the authority of this Henry de Lacy), had appropriated to the Castle eight years previously a piece of ground called *La Batailplace* (the Battle Piece), where wager of battle took place in appeals of felony, where the men of Lincoln were wont to play, the Friars to preach, and where other rights were enjoyed, and where the men of the country were wont, with carts and cattle, to have common passage to the city.

Henry de Lacy died in 1312 at his London mansion-nouse called Lincoln's Inn, and the Castle descended to his daughter Alesia (or Alice), wife of Thomas, Earl of Lancaster, grandson of King Henry III. The Earl of Lancaster, therefore, became Constable of the Castle in right of his wife, but, being executed for treason in 1322, his estates and dignities were forfeited to the Crown. Shortly afterwards Edward II restored to the widow, Alice, her ancestral inheritance, and when she contracted a second marriage with Ebulo le Strange, she had livery of Lincoln Castle; she died without issue in 1348, and her inheritance descended to her first husband's nephew, Henry, Earl of Lancaster, who was afterwards created Duke of Lancaster, and died in 1361. From him the Castle descended to his daughter Blanche, who became the wife of John of Gaunt.

Reversion to Crown and Purchase by County.

John of Gaunt's son, Henry of Bolingbroke, became King as Henry IV, and in his person the Constableship and fee of the Castle again became vested in the Crown, and so continued until the year 1831, when an Act of Parliament was passed enabling the County Magistrates to purchase the fee simple and inheritance of the Castle in trust for the benefit of the County of Lincoln. The deed of enfeoffment is dated 15th November, 1831, and the sum paid was £2,000.

County Prison.

The Castle having been thus far considered chiefly as a military stronghold, it remains to be stated that it was also the County prison. The Pipe Rolls of the reigns of Henry II and Richard I record divers payments for the provision of fetters, and bolts and bars for securing the prisoners, and in a Survey taken in 1606 it is stated that the Castle was used as a common gaol and that the Assizes had been held there "time out of mind."

Siege in Civil War.

After the outbreak of the Civil War in the time of Charles I, the Parliament, on the 9th January, 1643, issued an order for the removal of the prisoners to some secure place, and for the speedy strengthening of the fortifications of the Castle. From this it appears that the Parliamentarians were then in possession of the City, as they still were in July of the same year. Before October, however, the Royalists had ousted them, for in that month the Parliamentarians, under the Earl of Manchester, marched against Lincoln, made themselves masters of the place, and in the City, Close, and Minster captured arms for at least 2,500 men, 28 or 30 colours, three pieces of ordnance and great store of ammunition.

Early in 1644 the Royalists had once more regained possession of the city and the Castle, and in May of that year they were again attacked by the Earl of Manchester; he was again victorious, and, after taking the lower city, proceeded to assault the upper city and Castle, which presently surrendered to him. "Our men" (says an eye-witness, quoted by John Vicars, in his *God's Arke Overtopping the World's Waves*) "set up the Scaling ladders, which they in the Castle seeing, left their firing, and fell busily to throwing downe of great stones upon us, from over their works and walls, by which we received more hurt than by all their former shot, yet all would not daunt our men, but up to the top of the Ladders they got, which proved too short (many of them) to reach to the top of their walles and their workes, they being, most of them, as high as London walls, but yet they made shift to get up, which the enemy perceiving, they had no spirit now left in them, but betooke themselves to their heeles from the walls, and our men close following them, having all got over the walls and works, shouting, and hollowing, and following them as fast as they fled, but they not knowing whither to runne, cryed out for quarter, saying, they were poore array-men, and forced thither to fight." About 1,000 prisoners were taken including Sir Francis Fane, the Governor of Lincoln.

Soon after this siege the Castle again became a prison, and the extant evidence indicates that for the last two hundred and fifty years its sole uses have been connected with the trial, detention, and punishment of offenders.

Assize Courts and Prison Buildings.

Little is known of the extent or precise situation of the buildings in which the Courts of Assize were held or in which the prisoners were kept before the year 1787. In 1630 a "Prison for Women" was situate in the north of the Castle; in 1642 a certain dungeon within the Castle is described as "a nasty stinking place called the Witch Hole," and in 1652 the building wherein the Assizes and Quarter Sessions were holden is mentioned under the name of "the Shire House."

After the suppression of the rebellion in 1745, many of the captured rebels were confined within the Castle, and these were, in May, 1747, dispatched to Liverpool to be transported beyond the seas.

In 1787 the front or earlier portion of the existing prison was erected, Carr, of York, being the architect; and in 1845-6 this was altered and considerably enlarged under the direction of Messrs. Nicholson and Goddard, of Lincoln, architects, the outlay being nearly £14,000.

After the passing of the New Prisons Act, and upon the completion of the new gaol in Greetwell Road, the use of the old prison was, in 1878, discontinued. Until 1859 prisoners under sentence of death were publicly executed upon the roof of Cobb Hall; and from that date until 1877 the death penalty was inflicted at the southern end of the Assize Court buildings; the Keep contains the graves of many prisoners who were hanged at the Castle, and those also of debtors and others who died in gaol.

The County Hall and Assize Courts were erected between the years 1822 and 1826, from the design of Sir Robert Smirke, R.A., at a cost of upwards of £21,000; the furnishing and heating involved a further outlay of about £3,000. The new Courts were first used for the Assizes commencing March 7th, 1826, the presiding judges being Chief Justice Best and Justice Littledale. During the time of the erection of the new building, the Assizes were held in the Chapter House of the Cathedral.

Upon the walls of the Grand Jury Room in the County Hall are hung the portraits of:—The Right Honourable John Earl Brownlow, G.C.H., Lord Lieutenant and Custos Rotulorum, 1809 to 1852, (presented 1852); Sir Robert Sheffield, Bart., Chairman of Kirton in Lindsey Quarter Sessions, 1827 to 1856; The Right Honourable Charles Anderson Worsley, 2nd Lord Yarborough, Lord Lieutenant and Custos Rotulorum and Admiral of the County of Lincoln, M.P. for the County 1832 to 1835, M.P. for Lindsey, 1835 to 1846, (presented 1862); Charles Chaplin, Esq., of Blankney, M.P. for the County 1818-31, Chairman of Sleaford Quarter Sessions 1817 to 1859; Sir C. H. J. Anderson, Bart., Chairman of Lindsey Quarter Sessions, (presented 1873); Lord Kesteven, for 27 years M.P., Chairman of Kesteven Quarter Sessions; Lieut.-Colonel Weston Cracroft Amcotts, of Hackthorn, Vice-Chairman of Lindsey Quarter Sessions, (presented 1884). These pictures were subscribed for by the Magistrates and others and presented to the County.

Encroachments.

In olden days the Bail and a considerable domain above the Hill appertained to the Castle, but from time to time encroachments were made. Furthermore, the Crown made demises of various portions of the outlying premises to different persons; of these demises the most considerable was in the sixth year of Charles I, when the Battle Piece, the North Bale Dyke outside Newport Gate up to Hangman's Dyke, and many other parcels of property abutting upon or situate near the Castle, were granted to Charles Harbord and others.

In the year 1836 Philip Ball, of Lincoln, a brazier, who had acquired property near to the north-western angle of the Castle, was guilty of cutting away a considerable portion of the Castle mound, and this operation endangered the stability of the superincumbent wall. The County authorities thereupon interfered, and commenced proceedings in Chancery against the said Philip Ball, with the result that he was imprisoned for six months, and was only released upon paying a substantial sum towards the repair of the damage he had caused. It was during these operations that the Roman gateway mentioned on page 6 was discovered.

The Keep (Lucy Tower).

Printed by Libri Plureos GmbH in Hamburg, Germany